AF413603

CRACKING QUALITY

VAIBHAV DUBEY

ISBN
Paperback 979-8-89929-718-2
Hardcase 979-8-89961-264-0

Dedications...

To **Michael Scal**ia, my colleague, mentor, and enduring inspiration.

This book is a tribute to the wisdom you shared, the standards you raised, and the legacy you leave behind post-retirement.

With deep respect and gratitude.

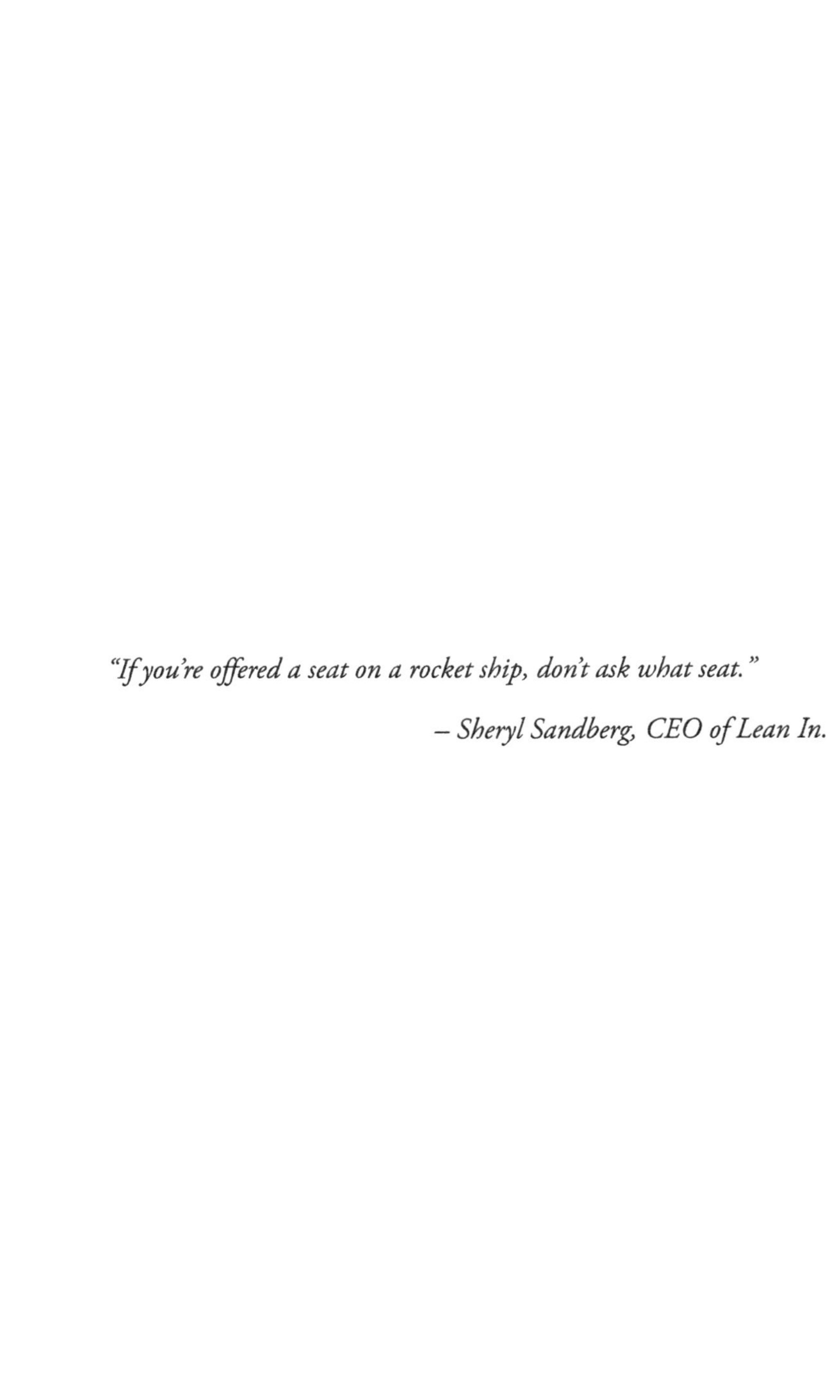

"If you're offered a seat on a rocket ship, don't ask what seat."

– Sheryl Sandberg, CEO of Lean In.

Contents

Book Review

In today's tech-driven world, speed is everything – but speed without 1uality is chaos. I've seen first-hand how the demand for innovation and velocity can often leave quality behind. But it doesn't have to be this way.

As a Mind Performance Coach and someone who works closely with high-performance professionals across industries, I understand the critical balance between moving fast and doing it right. This book bridges that gap with intelligence, foresight, and real-world strategies rooted in today's AI-driven reality.

Vaibhav brings nearly two decades of deep, practical experience in software quality and testing to this work—and it shows. He doesn't just explain what needs to change in the quality space, but also how to make those changes in real-world environments.

One of my favourite aspects of the book is how it ends—with a powerful bonus chapter that urges readers not just to learn but to act.

Vaibhav's insights will not only elevate how you test—but how you think about quality in everything you build.

Best wishes,

Manjunath MS

Mind Performance Coach | Author of *Unleash the Power of Reading*

Foreword

In an era where software evolves at lightning speed, the role of quality engineering has never been more crucial—or more complex. Today, we stand at the intersection of rapid development, low-code platforms, and the rise of artificial intelligence. It's here that Cracking Quality finds its purpose: guiding a new generation of testers and quality engineers to not just keep up with change, but to lead it.

This book was born out of both urgency and optimism. Urgency, because traditional testing practices are no longer sufficient in continuous integration and delivery pipelines. Optimism, because AI and low-code tools offer not just speed, but the opportunity to redefine quality itself—making it smarter, faster, and more human-centered than ever before.

Throughout these pages, you'll find practical strategies, real-world insights, and forward-thinking approaches to embedding AI into every corner of your quality engineering practice. Whether you're just beginning your career or looking to evolve your skills, this book is designed to meet you where you are—and help you rise.

Beyond the tools and techniques, this book is about a mindset. One that embraces experimentation, collaboration, and lifelong learning. A mindset where testers are not gatekeepers, but enablers of innovation and partners in delivering unbreakable software.

As the software world transforms, so too must the role of quality. Cracking Quality is your guide to navigating this transformation—boldly, intelligently, and with purpose.

For the next gen engineer, the future is not something to fear—it's something to crack wide open.

Let the quest begin.

*— **Dr. Aparajita Bhatt***
Associate Professor of Law
Director, Centre for Cyber Laws
Co-Director, Centre for Corporate Law & Governance
National Law University, Delhi

Preface

In today's software landscape, the pace of change is relentless. Release cycles that once spanned weeks or months have collapsed into days—or hours. Cloud-native platforms, microservices, and continuous integration/deployment (CI/CD) pipelines have made software delivery faster and more agile than ever before. However, with that speed comes complexity—and risk.

The question that keeps quality professionals up at night is this:

How do we ensure uncompromising quality at uncompromising speed?

This book was born from that very question.

Why This Book, and Why Now?

Cracking Quality: AI-Powered Testing for the Next-Gen Engineer is more than a guide to tools and techniques—it's a blueprint for how quality engineering must evolve in an age where AI, automation, and DevOps intersect.

For *fresh testers*, this book is your on-ramp into the future of testing. For *seasoned test professionals*, it's a reframing of your expertise through the lens of intelligent automation. For *test architects and engineering leaders*, it's a strategic playbook for scaling quality across fast-moving pipelines and cross-functional teams.

Software testing has already begun its transformation—from a reactive, manual gatekeeping activity to a proactive, continuous, and AI-augmented discipline. The role of the quality engineer is no longer confined to defect detection; it's expanding into quality advocacy, infrastructure design, observability, and intelligent decision-making.

Whether you are designing a CI/CD pipeline from scratch or modernizing a legacy testing strategy, this book will help you bridge the gap between where testing *has been* and where it's *going*.

What You'll Discover in These Pages

Each chapter is crafted to guide you step-by-step, blending technical insight with real-world relevance:

Chapter 1 – The Speed vs. Quality Paradox

Explore why traditional testing mindsets are breaking down in the face of modern delivery expectations, and why testing must evolve to remain relevant.

Chapter 2 – CI/CD Testing 2.0

Learn how artificial intelligence is redefining what it means to "shift left" and "shift right," and how test engineers can leverage AI for real-time, risk-based feedback.

Chapter 3 – Building a CI/CD-Ready Test Strategy

Build practical frameworks for embedding testing directly into the pipeline—from code commit to production deployment.

Chapter 4 – Continuous Feedback & Intelligent Test Analytics

Harness the power of data to optimize test coverage, identify flakiness, and align testing with business risk.

Chapter 5 – Overcoming CI/CD & AI Testing Challenges

Address the common hurdles in adopting intelligent testing, including cultural shifts, tooling gaps, and integration complexity.

Chapter 6 – AI-Powered Test Automation in Low-Code & No-Code Development

Discover how low-code platforms are reshaping who writes tests—and how AI can democratize automation for teams with diverse skill levels.

Chapter 7 – Security & Performance Testing in AI-Augmented Pipelines

Expand your scope of quality by integrating intelligent security scans and performance observability into your release workflows.

Chapter 8 – Resiliency Testing and Chaos Engineering in Low Code with AI

Get a glimpse of what's next: self-healing test suites, AI-generated tests, and the rise of autonomous QA agents.

Chapter 9 – The Future of Software Testing

Get a glimpse of what's next: self-healing test suites, AI-generated tests, and the rise of autonomous QA agents.

Chapter 10 – Becoming an AI-Driven Quality Engineer

Chart your personal and professional path toward mastering this new generation of testing. Whether you're hands-on or leading from the front, this chapter empowers you to drive quality transformation.

Chapter Timeless: The Time Is Now – Turning Quality Vision into Action – As a bonus, I have included a bonus chapter to provide inspirations to the readers to take massive actions. I urge the readers to spend some time to get apply the learnings to Cracking Quality!

Who This Book Is For

- **Early-career testers** looking to understand and grow with modern practices.

- **Experienced QA professionals** aiming to modernize their approach with AI and automation.

- **Test architects and DevOps leads** seeking scalable, intelligent strategies for end-to-end quality.

- **Developers and SDETs** interested in infusing AI into their testing toolkits.

The ideas in this book are grounded in real-world patterns, yet forward-looking enough to prepare you for what's ahead. Regardless of where you are in your testing journey, the time to evolve is now.

The tools may be changing, but the mission remains the same: **deliver better software, faster, and with confidence.**

Let's Crack Quality—together.

– Vaibhav
April 2025

Acknowledgements

To Kanchan and our kids for your love and warmth and for believing in me.

To my father and mother for your unwavering support and care.

To all my mentors, leaders, colleagues, and friends for inspiring me. Thanks, and gratitude to you.

Thanks to Dr. Aparajita Bhatt for the foreword. It means the whole world to me.

Special thanks to Padma Reddy, Narayan Bethmangalkar, Amy Gersema for your reviews, assistance and encouragement.

Heartfelt thanks to Dr Manjunath MS for expert guidance and the perfect book review.

To all my mentors, leaders, colleagues, and friends for inspiring me. Thanks, and gratitude to you.

Chapter 1
The Speed vs. Quality Paradox
Why Testing Must Evolve

"In the race for delivery, don't let speed trample trust."

— Anonymous

The Winners in Software Development would acknowledge the need to produce Quality Software. It's always about who gets there faster *(quoting the slogan from SoftwareAG WebMethods (now IBM)*: **Get There Faster**)!!

In today's fast-paced digital landscape, organizations strive to deliver software updates and new features swiftly to remain competitive. However, this acceleration often comes at the expense of thorough testing, leading to potential quality issues. This paradox—where the need for speed conflicts with the imperative for quality—poses significant challenges for software development teams.

Ensuring Quality has been an enticing and thrilling experience for the Quality Engineers. While a few would get a feeling of rushing through, few remain immersed in the moment when time stops.

Your general inquisitiveness is always the winner!

Would it be fun or an overwhelming experience? It depends upon the processes, tools, and practices you would adapt.

Your journey starts with understanding the Evolution of Software Development Practices.

Here's a basic flow of the journey:

• + CI/CD ———— • + GenAI ———— • and the journey continues...

+ DevOps • ——— Agile • ——— Waterfall

Initial software development followed the "Waterfall" model, characterized by sequential phases where testing occurred after development. This approach often led to late discovery of defects, making fixes costly and time-consuming.

The advent of Agile methodologies introduced iterative development, promoting continuous feedback and more frequent releases. Building upon Agile, DevOps emerged to further streamline the development pipeline by fostering collaboration between development and operations teams. The central theme of DevOps is CI/CD, which automates the integration and deployment processes, enabling rapid and reliable software delivery.

Challenges Posed by Modern Development Practices

The quest for Rapid Development and Delivery has led the organizations to innovate their processes.

While CI/CD and DevOps offer numerous benefits, they also present challenges for traditional testing approaches:

- **Increased Release Frequency:** With multiple deployments daily, manual testing becomes a bottleneck. With continuous integration and deployment, the expectations increase to produce production ready code at lightning speeds; from annual/bi-annual to on-demand releases.

- **Complex Environments:** Microservices architectures and cloud-native applications introduce intricate dependencies, complicating testing efforts.

- **Automation Demands:** There is a heightened need for automated testing to keep pace with rapid deployments. In fact, the automated suite must be able to complete very fast, should be stable and predictable.

There are enough examples to infer this paradox of Speed vs Quality.

1. **Boeing 737 Max Crashes**

   In 2018 and 2019, two fatal crashes involving Boeing's 737 Max aircraft resulted in 346 casualties. Investigations revealed that rushed software updates, inadequate testing, and oversight failures contributed to these tragedies. Whistleblower Ed Pierson highlighted safety concerns, emphasizing the dire consequences of prioritizing speed over thorough testing.

2. **Samsung Note 7 Disaster**

   The Galaxy Note 7 was a dual sim device with an elegant screen, an unparalleled camera and a nifty S-pen and it was so water-resistant it could reportedly withstand 30 minutes in the bathtub. However, in September 2016, Samsung announced a voluntary recall of their Note 7 devices citing faulty batteries. This infamous incident is a cautionary tale of what happens when speed is prioritized over quality. https://www.bbc.com/news/business-38714461

3. **Apple's iOS 8.0.1 Update**

   In 2014, Apple released the iOS 8.0.1 update to address specific issues but inadvertently introduced new problems, including loss of cellular service and Touch ID functionality. The hasty release without comprehensive testing led to widespread user dissatisfaction, highlighting the risks of insufficient testing in rapid deployment scenarios.

   You would ponder on what the way forward is to champion this paradox.

   Well, here are a few time-tested and powerful suggestions.

Adapting Testing Strategies for Modern Technologies

An inquisitiveness to adopt modern technologies is crucial. It's all about affirming yourself – that you have immense potential to master these skills.

Embrace Automation:

Develop proficiency in automated testing tools and frameworks to handle the demands of CI/CD pipelines. I was at awe, when I first encountered an automation tool and saw it as a magical world. It was IBM's Rational Robot Test Automation Framework. In due course, I came across many more frameworks. I witnessed creating our own automation framework.

Tip for you is to keep looking into how automation works.
Get into "How" it automates v/s "What" it does.

Understand DevOps Practices

Gain insights into DevOps culture to align testing strategies with development and operations workflows. Yet another magical ecosystem which included Operations with Software Development is DevOps.

You must experience the power of DevOps tools, Docker, Kubernetes and more. Once you develop a taste, you would appreciate the power of efficiency it brings in. The magical experience for me was to witness the speed of 'building and deploying' our changes to production.

Leverage AI and Machine Learning

Utilize AI-driven testing tools to predict potential defects and optimize test coverage. Friends, AI is already standing strong for the next decade. You must make friends with the AI tools. Get along LLM models, Machine Learning concepts and leverage them efficiently as your assistant in improving quality of your software. We will discuss in depth on the tools and tips on AI in the coming chapters.

Focus on Continuous Learning

Stay updated with emerging technologies and methodologies to remain relevant in the evolving landscape.

Being part of a community definitely helps. Start appreciating new techniques – presented in forums, articles, tech magazines, tech talks. Start enquiring on how does an AI generated Test Strategy looks? Check it out on how you would generate your test scenarios using AI tools. Start blogging, posting your opinions on articles, as it is *"learning in action."* Ask specific questions and you would get your answers!

Quality is free, but only to those who are willing to pay heavily for it."

— Peopleware

Chapter 2
CI/CD Testing 2.0

Integrating AI for Faster, Smarter Quality

"Artificial intelligence and generative AI may be the most important technology of any lifetime."

– Marck Benioff,

(chair, CEO, and co-founder, Salesforce)

Waterfall to DevOps: How Testing Has Transformed

Software testing has undergone a dramatic transformation over the past few decades. In the traditional **Waterfall** model, testing was a late-stage process done only after completion of the development cycle. This approach led to significant delays, as defects were discovered often too late, requiring costly rework.

There must have been instances when the Quality Teams would have held back from a scheduled release due to unacceptable technical debts.

The shift to Agile methodologies brought about continuous feedback loops, ensuring that testing was no longer an afterthought. Agile encouraged iterative development, where testing was performed throughout the software lifecycle. However, even Agile had limitations, as teams struggled to keep up with frequent releases and complex integrations.

Enter DevOps and CI/CD (Continuous Integration/Continuous Deployment), revolutionizing software development by automating testing, deployment, and monitoring. In this new paradigm, testing needed to become faster and cleverer to keep up with multiple daily deployments. However, as CI/CD pipelines grew in complexity, even traditional automation testing began to show its limitations.

The Bottlenecks in CI/CD Testing

Faster Testing and Development came with immense promises, but it was soon discovered that there were bottlenecks.

As we know the promise of Agile is "To get to the problems earlier!!"

There were broadly a few bottlenecks exposed in the process.

1. **Flaky Tests:** Automated tests often fail due to minor environmental changes, making them unreliable.

2. **Test Maintenance Overload:** Frequent code updates lead to constant script modifications.

3. **Slow Feedback Loops:** Large test suites slow down releases, contradicting the goal of rapid delivery.

This is where AI-powered testing comes into play, making CI/CD intelligent, self-healing, and predictive.

CI/CD Testing Pipeline Essentials – Key Stages for Modern Testing

A robust CI/CD pipeline integrates testing into every phase of the software delivery lifecycle. The key stages include:

1. **Build Verification Testing**

   Before new code enters the pipeline, smoke tests and static code analysis ensure that most issues are detected early. AI can enhance this step by identifying patterns in past build failures to predict potential defects before they occur.

2. **Automated Testing at Multiple Levels**

   • Unit Testing: Fast and isolated tests that verify individual components.

- Integration Testing: Ensures different modules interact correctly.

- End-to-End Testing: Validates complete workflows from start to finish.

AI's Role:

- AI-driven test case generation identifies the most critical paths.

- Self-healing automation fixes broken scripts without human intervention.

3. **Canary Releases and Progressive Deployment**

   Rather than deploying updates to all users simultaneously, canary releases deploy changes to a small subset first, minimizing risk. Feature flags allow teams to control feature rollouts dynamically.

   AI's Role:

- Real-time monitoring and anomaly detection predict potential failures based on user behaviour.

- AI-powered observability tools identify which deployments may cause regressions.

AI in CI/CD Pipelines – Smarter, Self-Healing Testing

We have witnessed various innovation events and challenges, with the winners always standing out with a niche in AI and ML topics.

Here are three powerful applications of AI to empower Software Quality Engineering:

1. **Self-Healing Test Automation**

    It was discovered that the initial test scripts were broken when UI elements changed, requiring constant maintenance.

    AI-powered test automation tools like **Applitools and Mabl** use *computer vision and machine learning* to adapt UI changes dynamically. You will 'experience the power' once you start making friends with these tools.

    It is well known that Google's AI-powered self-healing tests adapt to UI changes in Gmail and Google Docs, significantly reducing test maintenance.

2. **Defect Prediction and Risk-Based Testing**

    AI models analyse historical defect data and predict which areas of the code are most likely to break, which enables:

    Prioritization of high-risk test cases instead of running all tests.

    Reduced test execution time, making releases faster.

    IBM Watson AI analyses millions of test cases to recommend which ones to execute, cutting test execution time by 30%.

3. **AI-Powered Regression Testing**

    Regression testing ensures that new code does not break existing functionality. AI enhances regression testing by:

    – Detecting **flaky tests** and removing false positives.

    – Automatically updating test scripts based on code changes.

Real-World Examples – How Companies Use AI-Driven CI/CD Testing

Netflix – *Chaos Engineering & AI-Driven Observability*

Netflix had pioneered the deployment of hundreds of updates daily without downtime. Their AI-driven testing strategy includes the following:

- **Chaos Engineering** (Simian Army) to test system resilience.

- **AI-powered observability tools** detect performance issues before they impact users.

References:

Podcast WeAreNetflix: Episode 9 Chaos Engineering: https://www.youtube.com/watch?v=kxEZmfUFGJs

This concept has revolutionized Software Development and Delivery. Beautiful applications have merged to assist with chaos testing, e.g. Gremlin: https://www.gremlin.com/chaos-engineering

Google – *AI in Self-Healing Automation*

Google has exemplified its AI-driven approach towards CI/CD. The strategies include:

- Using machine learning models to detect flaky tests.

- Automation of test maintenance by self-healing UI test scripts.

- Leveraging AI-powered log analysis to identify failure patterns.

Amazon – *Predictive Defect Analysis in CI/CD*

Engineering teams at Amazon regressed upon integrating AI into its CI/CD pipelines to:

- ***Predict deployment failures based on previous defects***. Predictive defect analysis leverages historical data and machine learning models to identify high-risk areas in the codebase that are likely to fail. This approach aligns with the use of predictive analytics in CI/CD pipelines to anticipate deployment issues and improve software quality

- ***Optimize test execution by prioritizing risk-based testing***. Machine learning models such as *Amazon SageMaker and SageMaker AI* can prioritize high-risk code segments, enabling teams to focus their testing efforts on areas most prone to defects. This method is particularly effective in large-scale projects with limited testing resources

- ***Use automated rollback mechanisms when anomalies are detected***. Fully automated CI/CD pipelines, such as those advocated by Amazon Web Services (AWS), include mechanisms for quick fault isolation and rollback when anomalies or errors are detected during integration or deployment stages. This ensures minimal downtime and rapid recovery from failures

Conclusion: The Future of CI/CD Testing with AI

We are in the era of Testing 2.0 to unleash the power of CI/CD and AI. The following powerful takeaways must stick with you as food for thought.

Quality 2.0 with AI in CI / CD

Self Healing Automation

Defect Prediction & Risk-Based Analysis

Faster & Smarter Quality Assurance

In this journey of transformation, software testers must embrace AI-driven testing to stay ahead in the rapidly evolving world of CI/CD.

"Right now, people talk about being an AI company. There was a time after the iPhone App Store launch where people talked about being a mobile company. But no software company says they're a mobile company now because it'd be unthinkable to not have a mobile app. And it'll be unthinkable not to have intelligence integrated into every product and service. It'll just be an expected, obvious thing."

– Sam Altman, co-founder and CEO, OpenAI

Chapter 3

Building a CI/CD-Ready Test Strategy

"If you automate a mess, you get an automated mess"

– Rod Michael

In this fast-paced world of software development, achieving both speed and quality is the ultimate challenge. CI/CD pipelines have revolutionized how software is built, tested, and deployed, but without a solid testing strategy, they can lead to bottlenecks, flaky tests, and poor software quality. This chapter explores a structured approach to building a CI/CD-ready test strategy, leveraging AI, automation, and predictive analytics to test smarter, not harder.

Blueprint for "Test Smarter, Not Harder" – Balancing Speed and Quality

The Pitfall of Testing Everything

One common mistake in CI/CD is trying to test everything. While comprehensive test coverage is desirable, running thousands of tests for every small change slows deployment cycles and creates a maintenance burden. The solution is to optimize testing efforts—focusing on critical areas while leveraging AI-driven intelligence.

The Smarter Approach to CI/CD Testing

To achieve both speed and quality, a CI/CD-ready test strategy should consider the following steps:

- Prioritize high-risk areas instead of testing every line of code.

- Use automation effectively—but not blindly.

- Leverage AI-driven insights to optimize test selection and execution.

- Enable early defect detection to minimize post-release failures.

By shifting from a test-everything mindset to a risk-based, AI-assisted testing approach, organizations can increase testing efficiency without sacrificing software quality.

Continuous Testing: Why Test Execution is Not Enough

Continuous Testing is the practice of testing at every stage of the CI/CD pipeline, ensuring that defects are caught early and often. It involves:

- Pre-commit testing: Developers run quick unit and integration tests before pushing changes.

- Automated testing in CI/CD pipelines: Continuous execution of functional, API, security, and performance tests.

- Shift-right testing: Monitoring software in production using AI-driven observability tools.

Why Just Running Tests Isn't Enough?

Even with automation, traditional test execution doesn't guarantee quality. The real power of Continuous Testing comes from:

- Early risk detection: AI-driven analytics can predict high-risk areas before deployment.

- Intelligent test selection: AI can prioritize test execution based on code changes.

- Self-healing automation: AI-powered tools like Applitools and Mabl can detect UI changes and automatically fix broken test scripts.

By integrating AI-powered insights into Continuous Testing, teams can detect, prevent, and fix defects faster, reducing the need for post-release bug fixes.

The 80/20 Rule in Test Automation—Where to Invest for the Biggest ROI

The Problem with Over-Automation

Many teams invest too much time in automating everything, leading to:

- Flaky tests that break frequently.

- Slow test execution in CI/CD pipelines.

- Test maintenance overhead that wastes engineering time.

Applying the 80/20 Rule to Test Automation

The Pareto Principle (80/20 rule. Reference) suggests that 80% of defects come from 20% of the code. Instead of automating everything, focus automation efforts where they provide the highest ROI. We must understand that although automation is essential, it also adds to the burden of maintenance in future. Hence, we should be conscious on 'what' and 'what not' to automate.

What Should You Automate?

- Critical user journeys: Logins, payments, key workflows.

- APIs and back-end services: Faster and less flaky than UI automation.

- High-risk areas: Components that frequently change or have a history of defects.

- Performance and security testing: Detect bottlenecks before they impact users.

What Should You NOT Automate?

- Exploratory Testing: AI can assist, but human intuition is essential.

- Rarely used features: Focus on high-impact functionality.

- Tests that require frequent updates: Constant maintenance can be costly.

By focusing only on valuable test automation, teams can speed up CI/CD cycles while maintaining high quality.

AI-Assisted Test Case Generation: Using Predictive Analytics to Catch Defects Before They Happen

How AI is Revolutionizing Test Case Design

Traditional test case creation is manual and time-consuming. You may have used tools like excel to generate beautiful test cases, or even *TestRail, TestLink, qTest* etc. Well, testers consider this exercise as scientific and sacred, however, this involves good efforts and a process to review and improvise.

The way forward to revolutionize Test Case Generation is to leverage AI to automatically generate and prioritize test cases. AI-generated Test Cases would be based on:

- Historical defect data: AI identifies patterns in past failures.

- Code changes and risk analysis: AI predicts which areas of the application are most vulnerable.

- User behaviour analytics: AI models prioritize tests based on real-time user interactions.

Benefits of AI-Powered Test Generation

Saves time: Reduces the need for manual test case design.

Improves test coverage: AI-generated tests catch edge cases that humans might miss.

Reduces test maintenance: AI continuously updates test cases as the application evolves.

Google uses AI-driven testing in its CI/CD pipelines for products like Gmail and Google Docs (referenced here). Their AI-powered system:

Analyses past bugs to predict where new defects might occur.

Automatically generates test cases to cover new code changes.

Prioritizes test execution based on real-time risk assessment.

The Future of CI/CD Testing is AI-Driven

Building a CI/CD-ready test strategy requires a shift in mindset—from testing everything to testing smarter using AI and automation.

Leveraging AI-powered test case generation, young software testers can work smarter, reduce redundant testing, and improve software reliability.

By combining CI/CD automation with AI-driven intelligence, engineering teams can deliver high-quality software at lightning speed—without getting stuck in traditional testing bottlenecks.

"It is not the strongest of the species that survive, nor the most intelligent, but the one most responsive to change."

– Professor Leon C. Megginson
(paraphrased from Darwin's Origin of Species)

Chapter 4

Continuous Feedback & Intelligent Test Analytics

Some people call this artificial intelligence, but the reality is this technology will enhance us. So instead of artificial intelligence, I think we'll augment our intelligence.

– Ginni Rometty,

(Former CEO of IBM and author of Good Power)

In modern software development, quality assurance (QA) is no longer just about running test cases and checking pass/fail results. Instead, AI-powered analytics, continuous feedback loops, and intelligent automation have revolutionized testing. We will explore on how AI-driven insights, predictive analytics, and automated defect triaging can enhance quality engineering in CI/CD pipelines.

Why Traditional Testing Metrics Fall Short?

In legacy software testing practices, teams rely on:

- Pass/Fail Test Results – A test either works or fails but doesn't indicate risk trends.

- Defect Count – More bugs don't necessarily mean lower quality, severity matters.

- Test Coverage – Even 90% test coverage doesn't guarantee high-quality software.

On a contrary, AI-Driven Smart Test Metrics, empowers the engineering teams to produce better results with efficiency.

With AI-powered analytics, testing has shifted from binary results to risk-based intelligence. Leveraging the AI tools, teams are enabled to improve the test analytics in the following ways:

- Defect Risk Scoring – To prioritize test cases based on past failures.

- Flaky Test Detection – Identify unstable tests that randomly fail.

- Test Impact Analysis – Predict which tests are crucial for recent code changes.

We should take inferences from *Google's AI-Based Test Intelligence*.

Google has integrated AI-driven test impact analysis in its CI/CD pipeline for Gmail and Google Drive. Instead of running all tests, Google's AI engine analyses recent code changes and executes only relevant tests, significantly reducing test execution time. *(Check this article for reference)*

Seem's simple, isn't it? Just as an anecdote, the Quality Engineering teams across organizations would have spent enormous hours to solve this problem of intelligent test analysis. They would have been successful to some extent. However, Google had published this art, included in the AI models and frameworks.

Let's dive into 3 powerful and practical applications of leveraging AI in Software Quality Engineering:

- "Predictive Analysis in Testing"

- Intelligent Bug Triage & Root Cause Analysis

- Optimizing CI/CD with Smart Test Reporting

1. AI-powered predictive analytics uses historical data to forecast future failures.

Machine learning models analyse:

- Code changes and historical defects to predict areas most likely to break.

- Test execution patterns to detect slow, flaky, or redundant tests.

- User behaviour insights to determine high-risk functionalities.

Example: IBM Watson Predictive Testing

IBM uses AI-powered Watson Analytics to predict software defects before deployment. By analysing millions of historical test cases and bug reports, Watson prioritizes high-risk areas, improving defect detection rates by 30%.

Take a look at: IBM uses AI In Software Development.

2. Intelligent Bug Triage & Root Cause Analysis – Automating Defect Classification with AI

With a mindset of a Quality Engineering professional, you would have or soon encountered Bug Triaging and RCA (Root Cause Analysis). I would consider it is the best way for *Kaizen* (continuous improvement); however, one should discover following challenges during the process and compliment the power of AI in solving this puzzle.

Consider the following challenges faced in Manual Bug Triage:

- Duplicate Defect Reports – QA teams spend time reviewing redundant bug reports.

- Slow Defect Classification – Testers manually tag defects based on severity.

- Root Cause Uncertainty – Diagnosing defect origins can take days or weeks.

- With the above challenges in the manual process, here is how AI can Automate Defect Triage & Root Cause Analysis:

- Natural Language Processing (NLP): AI scans defect descriptions and automatically assigns categories.

- Automated Defect Clustering: AI groups similar defects to prevent duplicates.

- Root Cause Prediction: AI correlates logs, test failures, and code changes to identify defect origins.

Example: Amazon's AI-Driven Defect Management

Amazon uses machine learning to analyse and classify defects across AWS services. AI automatically prioritizes urgent issues, significantly reducing the time-to-resolution.

Reference: Amazon uses AI to sport damaged products before shipping to customers

3. Optimizing CI/CD with Smart Test Reporting – Using AI-Generated Reports to Guide Quality Decisions

Test Reporting is integral to Quality Measurements Systems. It is evident that the professionals would feel the burden of manual involvement in preparing the test reports.

Here's why the existing Test Reports Are Ineffective:

- Lengthy PDFs with No Insights

- Static Pass/Fail Summaries

- No Real-Time Quality Feedback

And here's how AI-Generated Reports Improve Testing:

- Automated Root Cause Analysis – AI pinpoints failure sources instantly.

- Risk-Based Test Reporting – AI highlights high-risk areas needing urgent attention.

- Self-Healing Reports – AI auto-updates insights based on recent test executions.

Inferences: **Netflix's AI-Powered CI/CD Insights**

Netflix runs thousands of daily deployments and relies on AI-powered reporting. Their system *Detects test trends across multiple releases, generates real-time risk assessments* and *uses AI to optimize test execution strategies, reducing downtime.*

Reference: Netflix TechBlog on Data Pipelines

Conclusion

By embracing AI-powered test analytics, software testers can move beyond reactive testing and build predictive, self-improving quality engineering systems.

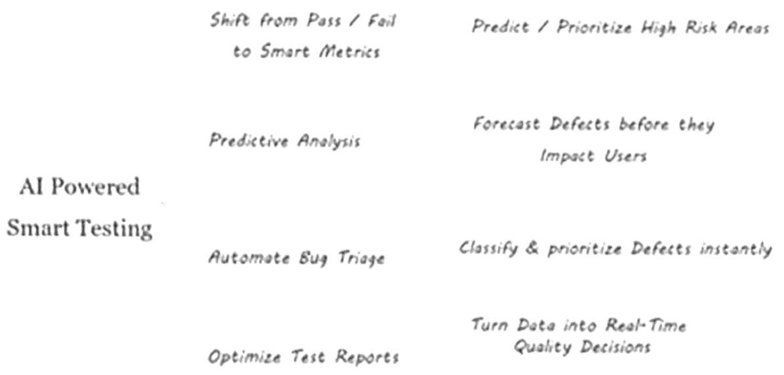

AI Powered Smart Testing

Chapter 5
Overcoming CI/CD & AI Testing Challenges

Dig into every industry, and you'll find AI changing the nature of work.

–DANIELA RUS

Director of MIT's Computer Science and Artificial Intelligence Laboratory.

Continuous Integration/Continuous Deployment (CI/CD) pipelines and AI-powered testing have transformed how software is developed, tested, and delivered. However, despite these advancements, organizations face several challenges in implementing and scaling AI-driven testing within CI/CD. Flaky tests, AI biases, security gaps, and deployment hurdles often slow down the adoption of AI in testing.

We will now explore the biggest challenges in CI/CD and AI-driven testing and practical solutions to overcome them.

The 3 most common challenges are *"Flaky Tests", "False Positives", and "Alert Fatigue".*

The Problem with Flaky Tests

Flaky tests are automated tests that fail intermittently, even when no defects exist. This inconsistency leads to wasted debugging time, broken pipelines, and a loss of trust in test automation.

On further brainstorming, the Most Common Causes of Flaky Tests are:

- Timing Issues – Race conditions where a test executes before a system is fully ready.

- Test Data Dependencies – Tests relying on dynamic data that change unpredictably.

- Environmental Differences – Variations in network latency, cloud infrastructure, or test environments.

Mitigating Flaky Tests:

- Implement Self-Healing Tests – AI-powered automation tools like Applitools, Mabl, and TestRigor can auto-adjust test scripts when UI changes occur.

- Use Retry Logic & Adaptive Waits – Instead of fixed delays, use intelligent waiting mechanisms (e.g., wait until an API response is received).

- Parallel Execution in Isolated Environments – Running tests in clean, containerized environments (Docker, Kubernetes) reduces interference.

Example: How ContextQA Reduced Flaky Tests using IBM's watsonx.ai The AI-powered test suites in the CI/CD pipelines makes the system efficient by implementing: -

- AI-powered self-healing test scripts that adapt to UI updates.

- Automated root cause analysis to detect and eliminate false positives.

- AI-driven test prioritization, considerably reducing test execution times.

AI Bias & Ethical Testing – Ensuring Fairness and Accuracy in AI-Driven Testing

Understanding AI Bias in Software Testing

It is well known that AI-powered content relies on machine learning models trained on historical data. However, if the training data contains inherent biases, AI models can reinforce unfair patterns in test results.

The following are the most common types of Bias in AI-Driven Testing:

- Data Bias – Training models on outdated or non-representative data leads to incorrect defect detection.

- Algorithmic Bias – AI models favour certain outcomes over others due to flawed logic.

- Automation Bias – Over-reliance on AI recommendations without human validation.

As a classic example of the Applicant Tracking System used at Amazon, they responsibly stopped using a hiring algorithm after finding it favoured applicants based on words like "executed" or "captured," which were more commonly found on men's resumes. The inherent issues were observed with natural language processing algorithms that can produce biased results within applicant tracking systems.

Strategies to Mitigate AI Bias in Testing:

- Diverse & Representative Training Data – Ensure AI models are trained on a wide variety of test scenarios, environments, and edge cases.

- Regular Bias Audits – Monitor AI-driven test decisions for inconsistent defect classification.

- Human-in-the-Loop Testing – Combine AI automation with human oversight to correct misclassified test results.

Example: IBM Watson's Approach to AI Bias in Software Testing

IBM incorporates AI fairness checks into its AI-driven testing tools. The Watson AI team regularly audits training data to identify bias patterns and ensures manual review of AI-generated test reports before deployment.

Security & Performance in CI/CD Pipelines – Why AI Alone Isn't Enough for End-to-End Quality

Security Testing Challenges in CI/CD

The need of the hour has always been faster deliveries and time to market. As we have now established that AI-driven approach stands as a game-changer, there are however a few anomalies.

- Fast Releases Create Security Gaps – Speed in CI/CD pipelines often leads to missed vulnerabilities.

- Automated Security Tests Are Limited – AI-driven security testing can detect known vulnerabilities but may struggle with zero-day exploits.

We thus need to understand the Best Practices for 'Secure CI/CD Pipelines'. The three most popular strategies are as follows:

- Shift-Left Security Testing – Embed security checks early in development using SAST (Static Application Security Testing) and DAST (Dynamic Application Security Testing).

- AI-Powered Threat Detection – AI-based tools like Darktrace analyse network traffic to detect anomalies and security threats in real time.

- DevSecOps Culture – Ensure testers, developers, and security teams collaborate to integrate security into CI/CD workflows.

Performance Testing Challenges in AI-Augmented CI/CD

Microservices & Cloud Complexity – Applications run on distributed cloud services that require continuous performance monitoring.

For instance, the existing load tests don't account for real-world user behaviour, however, AI-powered performance testing simulates dynamic user interactions.

As a real-time example, Amazon uses AI-powered observability tools like AWS DevOps Guru, and GuardDuty to:

Monitor real-time security threats, Optimize API performance by auto-detecting slow response patterns, and Automate security compliance testing for cloud-based services.

Scaling AI in Testing: From POC to Production – Practical Steps for Real-World Adoption

Let's understand a few key challenges of Scaling AI in Software Testing.

Proof-of-Concept (POC) vs. Full-Scale AI Adoption – Many companies struggle to move from AI test pilots to full implementation in CI/CD pipelines.

Data Limitations – AI models require large, high-quality datasets to function effectively. This remains as a challenge to leverage the full potential of LLM and analytics for business use as compared to initial POCs.

Integration with DevOps Toolchains – AI-based testing solutions must work seamlessly with tools like Jenkins, GitHub Actions, Selenium, and Kubernetes. The challenge lies in integrating the AI based solutions with the DevOPs infrastructure. The issue here is always in designing the infrastructure – where the existing frameworks were designed years back and now integrating with the AI solutions require massive re-designing and efforts.

Practical Steps to Scale AI in Testing

As the famous quote from the book Atomic Habits says: *"Success is the product of daily habits — not once-in-a-lifetime transformations."*

Taking inferences from the book "Atomic Habits" (by James Clear), the practical step to scale big is to start small!

Consider the following strategies to grow and leverage AI in Testing:

Start Small & Iterate – Deploy AI-powered test automation on a single project before scaling.

Leverage AI-Driven Test Orchestration – Tools like Launchable and Test.ai prioritize which tests to run, optimizing CI/CD efficiency.

Train Testers on AI-Augmented Testing – Upskill QA teams to work alongside AI, rather than replace manual testing.

Taking an example from this article on Netflix and its video streaming services. They had successfully implemented AI-powered test automation in their video streaming services.

Leverage AI to Detect UI Changes — To Adapt Test Scripts Automatically

Overcome Challenges in AI Testing

Employ Machine Learning — To Predict Outages before they Impact Users

Scale AI-Analytics — To Enhance CI / CD Pipelines

The Future of CI/CD & AI Testing

By proactively addressing flaky tests, AI bias, security gaps, and deployment challenges, organizations can maximize the value of AI-powered testing and build reliable, scalable CI/CD pipelines.

Chapter 6

AI-Powered Test Automation in Low-Code & No-Code Development

Ensuring Quality in a World Where Anyone Can Build Software

"Low code combined with AI will become even more valuable and safer."

– STARTECHUP

The rise of low-code and no-code (LCNC) platforms has revolutionized software development. Organizations are rapidly adopting platforms like Microsoft Power Apps, Mendix, OutSystems, and Appian to accelerate application development and reduce dependencies on traditional coding. While this shift speeds up delivery, it also introduces new challenges in software testing, as applications are built by non-technical users who may not follow best practices in quality assurance. According to Gartner, it's predicted that by 2026, about 80% of low-code development tool users will be developers from non-traditional IT departments.

To address these challenges, AI-powered test automation is emerging as the key enabler of quality in LCNC environments. AI-driven testing ensures that applications remain functional, secure, and scalable, even when developed by citizen developers with minimal coding expertise.

The Rise of Low-Code/No-Code Platforms and Their Impact on Software Testing

What are Low-Code and No-Code Platforms?

Low-code and no-code platforms enable users to create applications through drag-and-drop interfaces, visual workflows, and pre-built templates, significantly reducing the need for manual coding.

This empowers non-IT users to also create applications without prior coding experience. Thus "Citizen Developers," emerged as a new term coined by industry experts.

There are already a few platforms to help "Citizen Developers" create software applications utilizing the power of LCNC *(Low Code No Code)* platforms:

- **Microsoft Power Apps** – Helps businesses build apps with minimal coding efforts.

- **Mendix** – A platform designed for rapid application development with built-in automation.

- **OutSystems** – Offers full-stack development with AI-driven enhancements.

- **Appian** – Specializes in business process automation with minimal coding.

Impact on Software Testing

With the advent of LCNC revolution, Software Testing has become more challenging. Considering the "Citizen Developers", have less experience on engineering design patterns and coding standards, the onus lies on the underlying infrastructure to ensure quality. This makes testing even more challenging.

These hurdles include:

Increased Test Complexity – Since applications are built with pre-defined components, testing must validate both custom logic and platform limitations.

Frequent and Rapid Releases – Updates to the underlying LCNC platform can impact application behaviour, requiring continuous testing.

Limited Access to Code – Traditional test automation tools often rely on accessing source code, which is restricted in LCNC platforms.

Thus, need for AI-powered test automations would become essential to overcome these challenges.

Let's take a dive to explore different dimensions of AI-Powered Testing in Low Code Environments.

Self-Healing Test Automation

You would surely get a taste of flaky tests in UI automations. On top of this, the UI elements keep changing time and again – requiring the QA teams to adapt and enhance our automation scripts.

What if I say, there is already an AI-powered system to detect changes in UI and adapt the automation scripts automatically!!

IBM's AI-driven functional automation framework is for our rescue. This helps business and engineers maintain test stability when the UI elements change.

AI-driven Test Generation:

This one is simple, as the name suggests. Microsoft Power Automate, can record user workflows, and automatically create tests for common scenarios.

Visual Recording and Object Recognition

Using AI, we can identify visual elements on a page and validate their placement, ensuring consistency across different devices and screen sizes.

Tools like Applitools and Testim use AI for visual regression testing, ensuring that UI updates don't introduce visual defects.

The Quest for empowering Quality with AI has been ongoing for past decades. With the advent of powerful systems and machines, it is now possible for the world to leverage this technology.

There have been various case studies across organizations where engineering teams have tried to quench their thrust for Quality with AI.

How Microsoft Power Apps, Mendix, and OutSystems Handle Quality in Low-Code CI/CD Pipelines.

Case Study 1: Microsoft Power Apps – AI-Powered Test Automation

Microsoft Power Apps is widely used to develop enterprise-grade applications with minimal coding. To ensure quality at scale, Microsoft provides:

- Power Apps Test Studio – Allows users to create automated UI tests.

- AI-assisted bug detection – Microsoft's AI-powered analytics help identify potential application defects before deployment.

As a practical usage, a retail company used Power Apps to build an internal order management system. AI-driven testing ensured that workflow automation functioned correctly across multiple departments.

Case Study 2: Mendix – AI-Powered Testing in Agile Development

Mendix integrates AI-driven testing within its low-code development environment to help developers build, test, and deploy applications efficiently.

- Automated Test Generation – AI analyses application logic to suggest test cases.

- Self-Healing Scripts – Tests dynamically adapt to UI changes, reducing maintenance efforts.

- AI-Powered Performance Testing – Simulates real-world user traffic to prevent performance bottlenecks.

Example: A financial services company used Mendix to build a client onboarding system. AI-assisted test automation considerably reduced defects, ensuring seamless integration with legacy banking systems.

Case Study 3: OutSystems – CI/CD and AI-Enhanced Testing

OutSystems integrates AI-powered test automation within its continuous integration/continuous deployment (CI/CD) pipeline to improve software quality.

- Automated Regression Testing – AI monitors previous application versions and detects breaking changes.

- Predictive Failure Analysis – AI predicts potential failures before they impact production.

- CI/CD Optimization – AI identifies bottlenecks in testing cycles, accelerating releases.

Example: A healthcare provider built a telemedicine app using OutSystems. AI-driven testing ensured compliance with HIPAA security standards, preventing security vulnerabilities in sensitive patient data.

The Future of AI-Powered Testing in Low-Code Development

The adoption of low-code and no-code platforms is set to grow exponentially, making AI-powered test automation a necessity rather than an option. As businesses continue to rely on these platforms for rapid innovation, AI-driven testing will play a key role in ensuring software quality, security, and performance.

AI Test Automation:

Where Anyone can

Develop

By embracing AI-powered test automation, companies can accelerate development without sacrificing quality in their low-code/no-code applications.

Chapter 7

Security & Performances Testing in AI Augmented CI/CD Pipelines

Why AI Alone Isn't Enough for End-to-End Software Quality

"Is artificial intelligence less than our intelligence?"

– Spike Jonze

In the modern software development landscape, CI/CD pipelines have accelerated software delivery, but with speed comes the critical challenge of maintaining security and performance. AI has emerged as a powerful tool in testing, but relying on AI alone is not sufficient for end-to-end quality. Security threats evolve rapidly, and performance bottlenecks can cripple even the most well-designed applications. This chapter explores how AI augments security and performance testing while emphasizing the importance of DevSecOps and continuous validation.

The Role of AI in Security Testing – AI-Powered Vulnerability Scanning and Real-Time Security Monitoring

Security breaches can have devastating consequences, ranging from data leaks to complete system compromise. Traditional security testing methods often struggle to keep up with rapidly evolving threats.

AI-driven security testing enhances detection, prevention, and response by leveraging AI-Powered Vulnerability Scanning. These models include:

- **Automated Threat Detection:** AI models analyse vast datasets to identify vulnerabilities in applications and infrastructure.

- **Real-Time Code Analysis:** Tools, such as Checkmarx and Synk, continuously scan code repositories for security loopholes before deployment.

- **Self-Learning Threat Models:** AI adapts to emerging threats by analysing attack patterns and predicting potential security risks.

*These concepts are elaborated in the paper "Integrating AI-Based Security Into CI/CD Pipelines," *(published by BIPIN GAJBHIYE, Independent Researcher, Johns Hopkins University: **https://ijcrt.org/ papers/IJCRT2104743.pdf**)*

IBM's Watsonx for Cybersecurity leverages AI to analyse millions of security documents and threat reports, reducing false positives and identifying hidden threats. By integrating AI-powered security analysis into CI/CD pipelines, companies can detect and resolve vulnerabilities before they reach production.

AI-Driven Performance Testing: Detect & Prevent Failures before they occur

Performance issues can degrade user experience and lead to financial losses. Traditional performance testing often relies on predefined test scenarios. AI enhances performance testing in several ways.

Taking cues from Predictive Performance Analysis, which includes:

- **AI-Based Load Testing:** Tools like Apache JMeter integrated with AI can analyse historical performance data and predict future system behaviour under stress.

- **Anomaly Detection:** AI identifies deviations from normal system behaviour, preventing potential crashes and slowdowns.

- **Self-Optimizing Performance Tests:** Machine learning algorithms adapt testing scenarios based on real-world traffic patterns.

*These methodologies are detailed in the article "How AI Enhances Performance Engineering in DevOps and CI/CD Pipelines". https://

statusneo.com/how-ai-enhances-performance-engineering-in-devops-and-ci-cd-pipelines/

Case Study: Netflix's AI-Driven Chaos Engineering

Netflix employs Chaos Monkey, an AI-driven tool that randomly terminates services in its cloud infrastructure to test system resilience. This ensures that failures do not disrupt the user experience, improving overall system performance and reliability.

The Importance of DevSecOps and Continuous Security Validation in CI/CD

While AI-driven testing improves efficiency, security must be an ongoing process integrated into DevOps practices—known as **DevSecOps**. This approach ensures that security is embedded throughout the development lifecycle rather than treated as an afterthought.

This is not a new concept where the engineering teams deploys methods to ensure security in the Software Applications. The principles for DevSecOps include:

- **Shift-Left Security:** Security testing begins in early development stages rather than being delayed until deployment. By following the process, software teams can prevent undetected security issues when they build the application.

- **Continuous Security Validation:** AI-driven tools continuously monitor and test applications for vulnerabilities. DevSecOps teams might need to make multiple revisions in a day. To do that, they need to integrate security scanning tools into the CI/CD process. This prevents security evaluations from slowing down development.

- Automated Security Tools: DevSecOps teams might need to make multiple revisions in a day. To do that, they need to integrate security scanning tools into the CI/CD process. This prevents security evaluations from slowing down development. Few DevSecOps tools in practice include:

- SAST: Static Application Security Testing - to analyse and find vulnerabilities in proprietary source code.

- SCA: Software Composition Analysis - a process of automating visibility into open-source software (OSS) use for the purpose of risk management, security, and license compliance

- IAST: Interactive Application Security Testing - to evaluate an application's potential vulnerabilities in the production environment. IAST consists of special security monitors that run from within the application.

- DAST: Dynamic Application Security Testing - to mimic hackers by testing the application's security from outside the network.

* These principles are discussed in "DevSecOps Principles and Key Steps for Securing the CI/CD Pipeline". https://hackernoon.com/devsecops-principles-and-key-steps-for-securing-the-cicd-pipeline

You may wonder, how would DevSecOps fit into the Agile Development practices. Well, they both are not mutually exclusive practices. With DevSecOps, the software team can produce safer code using agile development methods.

Google's Security-Focused DevSecOps Approach: BeyondCorp security

Google integrates security at every stage of development, using AI to detect vulnerabilities in code, automate compliance checks, and validate infrastructure security. Their **BeyondCorp** security model ensures that applications are secured by design, reducing the attack surface in

CI/CD environments. By shifting access controls from the network perimeter to individual users, BeyondCorp enables secure work from virtually any location without the need for a traditional VPN. It allows for single sign-on, access control policies, access proxy, and user-based and device-based authentication and authorization.

Conclusion

AI plays a crucial role in security and performance testing, but it is not a silver bullet. AI alone is not enough for end-to-end software quality. Security threats are constantly evolving, and performance bottlenecks can arise unexpectedly. Organizations must adopt a balanced approach that combines AI-driven testing with DevSecOps principles, continuous validation, and proactive threat mitigation. By integrating AI with human expertise, businesses can ensure that software is not only delivered at speed but also maintains the highest standards of security and performance.

Key Takeaways

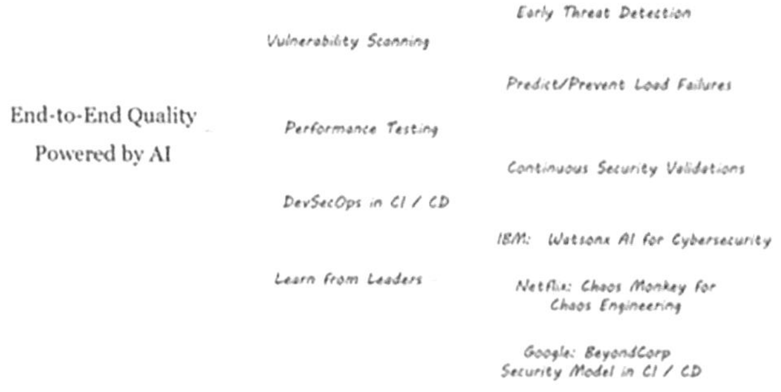

AI enhances security and performance testing, but true software quality comes from intelligent integration, strategic automation, and continuous monitoring. The future of CI/CD testing lies in combining AI's power with human judgment and robust security frameworks.

Chapter 8

Resilience Testing and Chaos Engineering in Low-Code with AI

The Rise of Resilience in the Quality Equation

"The real test is not whether you avoid this failure… but whether you let it harden or shame you into inaction, or whether you learn from it."

– Barack Obama

As enterprises increasingly adopt low-code platforms to accelerate software delivery, the expectations for quality have broadened. Traditional testing pillars—functional, regression, and performance testing—are no longer sufficient. In modern software ecosystems, resilience is emerging as a foundational quality attribute. This shift is fuelled by the reality that today's applications, even those developed in low-code environments, often operate within complex, distributed systems.

In this context, resilience refers to a system's ability to continue operating under adverse conditions—such as partial outages, delayed responses from third-party APIs, or unexpected data anomalies. Ensuring resilience in such conditions is no longer a luxury—it is a necessity.

Why Low-Code Still Needs Chaos

A common misconception is that low-code applications are inherently simpler and thus less prone to failure. While low-code platforms abstract much of the underlying architecture, the applications built on them still rely heavily on external services, APIs, and cloud infrastructure.

For instance, a customer onboarding app built in a low-code environment might depend on external identity verification (KYC) services, payment gateways, and customer relationship management systems.

If any of these components fail, the application could grind to a halt—unless it's resilient by design. That's where chaos engineering enters the picture.

Chaos engineering, a term popularized by Netflix's Chaos Monkey (*Basiri et al., 2016*), is the practice of injecting controlled failures into a system to observe how it responds and recovers. Its goal is to uncover systemic weaknesses before users experience them. Traditionally, chaos engineering required deep infrastructure control—difficult to achieve in low-code environments. However, AI is changing that narrative.

AI as the Catalyst for Resilience in Low-Code

Artificial Intelligence introduces a new dimension to resilience testing in low-code platforms. AI-powered quality engineering tools can simulate faults, predict failure points, and recommend or even automate recovery strategies—all without requiring access to infrastructure code.

Key AI-Driven Techniques Include

1. **Predictive Fault Modeling:** Using machine learning models trained on production logs and telemetry data, AI systems can predict which components are most likely to fail. This allows QA teams to focus resilience tests where they matter most.

2. **Synthetic Chaos Injection:** AI models can simulate realistic failure scenarios like high-latency API calls, missing database records, or corrupted responses from microservices. For example, a chatbot built using Microsoft Power Apps might encounter high error rates from a dependent language translation API. AI can simulate this degradation and assess how the application behaves under strain.

3. **Autonomous Anomaly Detection:** Rather than writing rules for every error scenario, AI models can detect anomalies in system behaviour, such as unusual memory usage, sudden latency spikes, or traffic drops, and flag them as early signs of failure.

4. **Self-Healing Recommendations:** By analysing historical incident patterns and code behaviour, AI can recommend fallback mechanisms—such as default values, retry logic, or asynchronous messaging—to improve recovery time without human intervention.

A Real-World Case

Resilient Onboarding Flow

Consider the case of a fintech company using a low-code platform like OutSystems to develop a digital onboarding journey. The workflow included integrations with:

- A third-party KYC verification service

- An internal CRM for customer data

- A cloud-based document storage system

To assess resilience, the team used an AI-driven testing tool (similar in capability to tools like Gremlin or LitmusChaos but adapted for low-code compatibility) to introduce synthetic failures.

The test scenarios included:

- Simulating a timeout from the KYC API

- Injecting corrupted payloads from the document storage system

- Blocking CRM access for a segment of transactions

The AI system observed that:

- The application lacked fallback messaging when the KYC service failed, leading to silent user drop-offs.

- Errors from the document system were not handled, crashing the workflow.

- CRM unavailability led to incorrect status updates downstream.

With these insights, the team applied changes using configuration-based error handling offered by the platform, rather than code rewrites. Additionally, the AI engine recommended retry strategies and asynchronous processing queues to ensure data consistency.

This example illustrates how resilience engineering can be achieved even in abstracted environments, provided AI is used effectively to simulate, detect, and guide improvements.

Building a Resilience Testing Pipeline in Low-Code CI/CD

Integrating resilience testing into a CI/CD pipeline in low-code environments is now possible with the help of AI. Here's a sample workflow:

1. **Pre-Deployment Risk Modeling:** AI models analyses changes and compares them to known failure patterns.

2. **Fault Scenario Generation:** Generation of custom chaos experiments based on new or changed components.

3. **Simulated Fault Execution:** During staging or test phases, injection of synthetic failures into workflows can be done using AI models.

4. **Observability and Response Monitoring:** Monitoring of the system's responses and flags resilience gaps.

5. **Automated Remediation Guidance:** Based on the observed behaviours, the AI model proposes remediation strategies such as retry logic, error suppression, and user notifications.

This approach is scalable and does not require heavy infrastructure investments—making it ideal for organizations embracing low-code at speed.

Benefits of AI-Driven Resilience Testing

- **Proactive Issue Discovery:** Catch weaknesses before users experience them.

- **Reduced Downtime:** Faster detection and automated recovery guidance.

- **Improved User Trust:** Applications that fail gracefully retain user confidence.

- **Operational Efficiency:** Fewer late-stage or post-production incidents.

Challenges and Ethical Considerations

While AI makes resilience testing more accessible, caution is required. Injecting chaos into production environments can be risky without proper safeguards. Ethical considerations, such as data privacy during simulated failures, must be respected—especially in regulated industries.

Moreover, AI models must be transparent and explainable to gain the trust of engineering and compliance teams.

Final Thoughts

AI-powered resilience testing is redefining how quality is measured and assured in low-code development.

By combining the philosophies of chaos engineering with the predictive and adaptive capabilities of AI, quality engineering teams can move from reactive firefighting to proactive defence.

Resilience Testing & Chaos Engineering

- AI-driven Techniques
  - Predictive Fault-Modelling
  - Synthetic Chaos Injection
  - Autonomous Anomaly Detection
  - Self-Healing Suggestions
- Build Pipelines for Resilience Testing
  - Pre-Deployment Risk Modeling
  - Fault Scenario Generation
  - Simulated Fault Execution
- The Benefits
  - Proactive Issue Discovery
  - Improved User Trust
  - Reduced Downtime
  - Operational Efficiency

In a world where outages can cost millions, and customer trust is hard to win back, resilience isn't just another non-functional requirement—it's a competitive advantage. And with AI at the helm, it's now within reach, even in the low-code world.

"You can't predict the future, but you can build a system that's prepared for it"

— Nora Jones, Chaos Engineering Pioneer and Founder of Jeli.io

Chapter 9

The Future of Software Testing

AI, Self-Healing Code, and Autonomous QA

The Next Era of Software Testing

"A good tester is a detective, not a robot"

— Jonathon Wright

As software development accelerates with lightening delivery expectations using CI/CD, Agile, and DevOps, the existing testing methods struggles to keep up. The next evolution of software testing is being shaped by AI-driven automation, self-healing code, and autonomous testing systems. This chapter explores how these innovations are transforming software quality assurance and what testers need to do to stay relevant.

AI-Powered Test Automation – Beyond Scripted Testing

Existing automated testing relies on scripted test cases, which require frequent maintenance with functional enhancements. Engineering teams around the globe would be well-known with the issue of Test Flakiness in the BVTs *(Automated Build Verification Tests).*

AI-driven test automation is revolutionizing creating and maintaining automation by concepts like:

Self-Adapting Test Cases

- AI can automatically generate and modify test scripts based on application changes, reducing test maintenance effort.

- Tools like Testim and Mabl use machine learning to adjust test cases dynamically when UI elements change.

Intelligent Test Selection

- Instead of running all tests, AI tools can analyse code changes and predict the highest-risk areas to test first.

As an example, Google uses AI-driven test prioritization to reduce execution time in its large-scale CI/CD pipeline.

The Rise of Self-Healing Code

Yet another powerful concept which engineering teams has been researching on is: "Self-Healing" in code, test, and business applications. Self-healing code is an emerging technology where **software detects and fixes its own defects without human intervention**. It is evident now that this challenge is well tackled using:

Automated Defect Resolution

- AI-powered debugging tools can identify the root cause of a failure and suggest or implement fixes.

Example: IBM's **Cloud Pak for Watson AIOps** analyses application logs and autonomously resolves issues before impacting users.

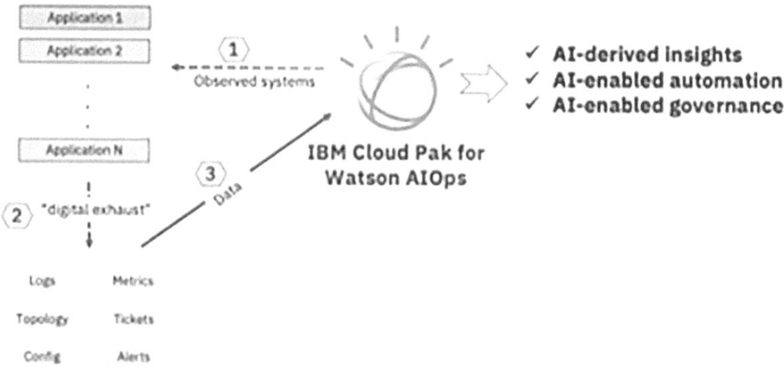

Image Courtesy: https://www.ibm.com/blog/aiops-a-path-to-reliability-at-cloud-scale/

Self-Healing Test Automation

- AI-driven tools can repair failing tests by identifying changes in the application and adapting assertions dynamically.

Applitools' Visual AI detects UI changes and updates tests without manual intervention.

Autonomous QA – The Future of Fully Automated Testing

The goal of AI in testing would be to create **autonomous QA systems** that require minimal human oversight. The future is striving towards a fully automated testing process.

We have discovered the BDD *(Behaviour Driven Development)*, TDD *(Test Driven Development)* concepts, and now AI-Driven Development (AIDD*) *The concept of AIDD is thoroughly mentioned across globe, for instance in this article on AI-Driven Development Glossary by Eric Elliot.*

The concept of a fully Autonomous QA Systems include:

AI-Driven Test Creation

Automatic Test Generations – where the AI Ecosystem either assists or drives the test generation based on user interactions and real-world behaviour.

As an example: Facebook's **Sapienz AI** generates and executes exploratory tests to detect potential failures in mobile apps.

Predictive Analytics for Defect Prevention

Looking at Amazon's AI-powered testing framework, which analyses the entire deployment history to anticipate risky releases.

An AI ecosystem that can churn the historical bug patterns and easily predict areas which are likely to contain defects, hence preventing failures before they occur.

How Testers Can Stay Relevant in the AI-Powered Future

In my opinion, Testers should leverage the AI-Powered ecosystems to assist their decision making on proving a bug with relevant arguments.

The happiness and satisfaction of exploratory testing would still stay relevant, and testers would continue enjoying this Art of Testing!!

However, in the journey ahead, we all should stay relevant and prepare ourselves to embrace the power of Generative AI.

As AI takes over repetitive testing tasks, the role of software testers is evolving. It is imperative that to stay ahead, testers should focus on a few key items:

- **AI-Augmented Testing Skills**: Learning how to work alongside AI-driven tools rather than relying on traditional scripting.

- **Exploratory and Ethical Testing**: While AI can automate many tasks, human intuition is still crucial for exploratory, security, and ethical testing.

- **Understanding AI & Machine Learning** Concepts: Testers should develop knowledge in AI algorithms to improve their ability to train and validate AI-driven test automation systems.

Conclusion

The future of software testing is AI-driven, self-healing, and autonomous. While these technologies will take over repetitive tasks, human testers will play a key role in guiding AI, ensuring ethical testing, and validating AI-generated results.

The Future of Software Testing

- AI-Powered Test Automation
  - Reduce Manual Efforts & Increase Efficiency
- Self-Healing Code
  - Detect & fix App Defects automatically
  - Self-Healing Test Automation
- Autonomous QA
  - AI-Driven Test Development
  - Predictive Analysis for Defect Prevention
- Tester's Power Notes
  - Learn AI-Augmented Testing Skills
  - Sharpen your Exploratory and Ethical Testing Skills
  - Train & Validate your own AI-driven Automation Systems

By embracing AI and continuously learning new skills, testers can future-proof their careers in this rapidly evolving landscape.

The pleasure in testing would remain in breaking the code!

Chapter 10
Becoming an AI-Driven Quality Engineer

Upskilling, Career Growth, and Future-Proofing Your Role in QA

"The path to success is to take massive, determined actions"

– Tony Robbins

The software testing landscape is undergoing a profound transformation with the rise of AI-augmented engineering. As software development accelerates through CI/CD pipelines, testers must evolve beyond traditional approaches to stay relevant. AI-powered automation, predictive analytics, and self-healing test frameworks are no longer futuristic concepts—they are the present and future of quality assurance.

This chapter presents a structured roadmap to help software testers transition into AI-powered testing, build essential skills, and future-proof their careers in an increasingly automated world.

Transitioning from Manual Testing to AI-Augmented Testing

Understanding the Shift

Manual testing, while essential in specific scenarios, is being rapidly supplemented and, in some cases, replaced by AI-driven approaches. Modern software testers must shift from executing test cases to designing AI-assisted strategies, leveraging machine learning models, and integrating automation frameworks.

Key Transformational Changes

- AI-driven test automation reduces human effort in repetitive tasks and enhances test accuracy.

- Self-healing test frameworks minimize maintenance overhead by dynamically adapting to UI changes.

- Predictive analytics in AI testing enables proactive defect identification, reducing post-deployment risks

Steps to Transition into AI-Augmented Testing

Transitioning into AI-powered testing requires a deliberate upskilling journey. Here's a structured approach to make the shift:

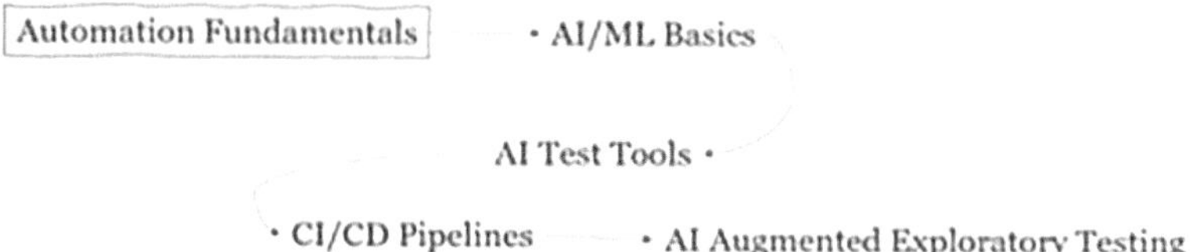

1. Master Automation Fundamentals – Start with industry-leading tools like Selenium, Cypress, or Playwright to understand core test automation principles.

2. Understand AI and Machine Learning Basics – Gain knowledge of AI concepts such as neural networks, predictive analytics, and anomaly detection to enhance testing strategies.

3. Experiment with AI-Powered Testing Tools – Hands-on experience with tools like Testim, Mabl, and Applitools will provide exposure to AI-driven automation.

4. Integrate Testing with CI/CD Pipelines – Learn how automated tests function within DevOps workflows using platforms like Jenkins, GitHub Actions, and Azure DevOps.

5. Apply AI-Augmented Exploratory Testing – Leverage AI insights to refine exploratory and performance testing strategies, improving efficiency and defect discovery rates.

Essential Skills for AI-Driven Quality Engineers

To remain competitive in the AI-powered DevOps ecosystem, software testers must develop a well-rounded skill set combining technical, analytical, and strategic capabilities.

1. AI & Automation Proficiency

   - Gain expertise in AI-powered testing frameworks that enhance test execution and defect prediction.

   - Strengthen test automation scripting skills using Python, Java, or JavaScript.

2. DevOps & CI/CD Integration

   - Master Shift-Left Testing principles to catch defects early in the development lifecycle.

   - Develop expertise in integrating automated tests into CI/CD pipelines for seamless deployments.

3. Cloud & Containerized Testing

   - Learn to test applications running in Docker, Kubernetes, AWS, and Azure environments.

   - Implement AI-driven performance monitoring for cloud-based applications.

4. Critical Thinking & Collaboration

   - Develop problem-solving skills to analyse AI-generated test reports effectively.

   - Strengthen collaboration with developers, DevOps teams, and AI model trainers to integrate AI-driven testing into agile workflows.

The Roadmap for Building a Career in AI-Powered Quality Engineering

At this juncture, you must chart your own journey towards mastering AI-driven quality engineering. Here's a five-step roadmap to accelerate your growth:

Step 1: Build a Strong Foundation in QA & Automation

- Deepen your knowledge of functional testing, test planning, and automation frameworks.

- Work on projects that involve AI-powered testing tools.

Step 2: Gain Hands-On Experience with AI-Driven Testing Tools

- Start with platforms like TestRigor, Functionize, or Applitools to understand AI-driven automation.

- Explore self-healing test automation and AI-based defect triaging.

Step 3: Engage with Open Source & AI Test Automation Communities

- Join forums such as TestGuild, Ministry of Testing, or contribute to GitHub open-source AI testing projects.

- Participate in AI and software testing hackathons to apply concepts in real-world scenarios.

Step 4: Earn AI & Testing Certifications

Consider certifications such as:

- ISTQB AI Testing Certification – To gain foundational AI testing knowledge.

- AWS Machine Learning Certification – To understand cloud-based AI implementations.

- Certified AI Automation Engineer (CAIAE) – For specialized AI automation skills.

Step 5: Specialize in AI-Augmented QA Engineering

- Focus on advanced areas like AI-powered security testing, AI-driven performance engineering, or predictive analytics for defect prevention.

Conclusion

The future of software testing belongs to AI-augmented quality engineers who can harness automation, predictive analytics, and self-healing test frameworks. By continuously upskilling in AI-driven testing strategies, DevOps automation, and cloud-based performance testing, testers can remain indispensable in the evolving software development landscape.

Act Now: *By embracing AI-powered testing, software testers can transition from traditional test execution roles to AI-driven quality engineering, ensuring their relevance in the era of autonomous testing.*

Chapter 11
Timeless!! The Time Is Now make changes everywhere

Turning Quality Vision into Action

"You don't have to be great to start, but you have to start to be great."

– Zig Ziglar

From Learning to Leading: Action Matters!!

Throughout this book, we've explored how AI and low-code platforms are reshaping the quality engineering landscape. From autonomous test generation to AI-powered chaos engineering, you're now equipped with both the strategies and the tools to thrive in this new era.

But knowledge without action is like a blueprint without construction—it holds potential, but no real-world impact.

This final chapter is a rallying call to turn insight into execution and learning into leadership. As Tony Robbins emphasizes in *Awaken the Giant Within,*

"It's not what we do once in a while that shapes our lives, but what we do consistently."

– (Robbins, 1991).

The same applies to software quality: the real transformation comes not from one initiative or test suite, but from repeated, deliberate practice and continuous improvement.

Why Consistency Outranks Intensity

In quality engineering, big initiatives often fail because they're treated as one-off projects. A team might introduce AI-based testing once but never update the models.

Or they might roll out a low-code app with a strong initial test strategy but never revisit it. True excellence is not built on intense, infrequent sprints—it is cultivated through small, consistent steps executed daily.

Motivational speaker Darren Hardy, in *The Compound Effect*, writes:

"Small, smart choices + consistency + time = radical difference."

– (Hardy, 2010)

Adopting AI in quality engineering doesn't require a massive overhaul overnight. Start small. Automate one test suite.

Run one AI analysis. Refactor one workflow. The compound effect will kick in sooner than you think.

Bridging the Intention-Action Gap

Despite best intentions, many professionals get stuck at the start line.

The gap between *knowing* and *doing* is where careers stall and innovation dies. Here's how to cross that gap with purpose:

1. **Start Before You're Ready**

   Perfectionism kills momentum. As Mel Robbins says in *"The 5 Second Rule"*:

   "You are never going to feel like it."

   – (Robbins, 2017)

Waiting for the "perfect moment" delays your growth. Whether it's launching an AI test bot or introducing predictive analytics in your CI/CD pipeline—start scrappy. Improve as you go.

2. **Break It Down**

   Overwhelm is often the result of unclear steps. Break your quality goals into small, manageable tasks:

- **This Week:** Pilot an AI tool on a small module

- **This Month:** Automate regression testing for a low-code app

- **This Quarter:** Train your team on AI-driven test strategy

3. **Track Progress, Not Perfection**

   Use metrics to track your learning and implementation efforts. Are tests running faster? Are bugs caught earlier? These signs of incremental progress are the building blocks of quality maturity.

Inspirations from the Field

Look at real-world teams that have embraced consistency over complexity:

- A mid-sized logistics company adopted AI-assisted testing for their Mendix low-code platform. They didn't aim to automate everything on day one. They started by automating user login tests. Within six months, they had 70% of their business-critical workflows covered with adaptive AI tests.

- A QA engineer at a startup used a no-code AI tool like Testim to identify flakiness in end-to-end tests. Instead of replacing all test cases, she fixed one daily. Over time, stability improved by over 60%.

Both examples show that you don't need a massive budget or a dedicated AI lab. What you need is consistency, curiosity, and commitment.

Building Your Personal Quality Roadmap

To turn inspiration into a personal mission, create a roadmap that aligns your day-to-day actions with long-term outcomes:

Time Frame	Action Item
Daily	Study new AI quality tools for 15 minutes
Weekly	Run a small-scale experiment on a project
Monthly	Present findings to your team
Quarterly	Evaluate and scale successful initiatives
Annually	Lead or contribute to a quality transformation

Think of it as your **"Quality GPS"**—you may take wrong turns or detours, but if you stay consistent, you'll arrive at your destination.

Creating a Culture of Action in Your Team

Success isn't a solo act. Bring your team along for the journey. Share insights from this book.

Start discussions around AI-powered testing in sprint retros. Encourage experimentation, reward learning, and normalize failures as steps toward innovation.

As John C. Maxwell writes in *"The 21 Irrefutable Laws of Leadership"*:

"A leader is one who knows the way, goes the way, and shows the way."

– (Maxwell, 2007)

You don't need a formal title to be that leader. Lead by action.

Final Words: From Reader to Change Agent

You've reached the end of this book, but you're standing at the beginning of a transformational journey. The future of quality engineering is not only automated and intelligent—it's *inspired*.

It's driven by people who are bold enough to take the first step and persistent enough to keep walking.

"Success is the sum of small efforts, repeated day in and day out."

— *Robert Collier*

Remember, you already have what it takes. The tools are here. The time is now. It's your turn to lead the way for…

"Cracking Quality !!"

Index

Chapter 1

Get There Faster (Slogan): https://www.sloganlist.com/technology-slogans/software-ag-slogan.html

Software Development Methods Timeline: https://www.researchgate.net/figure/Software-development-methods-timeline_fig3_275654650

Code Deployment Frequency: https://launchdarkly.com/blog/deployment-frequency/

Boeing 737 Max – Speed vs Quality Paradox:

https://www.nytimes.com/2024/03/28/business/boeing-quality-problems-speed.html

Samsung Galaxy Note 7 Disaster: https://www.techtarget.com/searchcio/news/450401154/Samsung-Note-7-disaster-a-CIO-parable-about-quality-assurance

https://www.bbc.com/news/business-38714461

The Volkswagen Scandal: https://www.bbc.com/news/business-34324772#:~:text=It's%20been%20dubbed%20the%20%22diesel,in%20Europe%20%2D%20including%20petrol%20vehicles.

Peopleware: Productive Projects and Teams https://en.wikipedia.org/wiki/Peopleware:_Productive_Projects_and_Teams

Chapter 2

https://www.ibm.com/products/blog/driving-quality-assurance-through-the-ibm-ignite-quality-platform

How is IBM leveraging GenAI to accelerate testing and improve Quality

https://www.youtube.com/watch?v=mRMumW-73DY

Netflix Chaos Engineering: Podcast

https://www.youtube.com/watch?v=kxEZmfUFGJs

Gremlin for Chaos Testing: https://www.gremlin.com/chaos-engineering

Google's AI-powered testing for gmail docs:

https://9to5google.com/2023/03/30/gmail-docs-ai-testing/

IBM Watsonx AI (Ignite Quality Platform IQP): https://www.ibm.com/products/blog/driving-quality-assurance-through-the-ibm-ignite-quality-platform

Inferences:

https://moldstud.com/articles/p-exploring-the-latest-trends-in-software-testing-and-quality-assurance-insights-and-innovations-for-2023

Gremlin: https://www.gremlin.com/chaos-engineering

Amazon SageMaker and SageMaker AI

Amazon – Prescriptive guidance for cicd: https://docs.aws.amazon.com/pdfs/prescriptive-guidance/latest/strategy-cicd-litmus/strategy-cicd-litmus.pdf

Chapter 3

AI powered CI/CD pipeline improves time to delivery at Google:

https://devops.com/ai-powered-devops-transforming-ci-cd-pipelines-for-intelligent-automation/#:~:text=Notably%2C%20Google%20uses%20AI%20to,as%20conducting%20activities%20become%20efficient.

Pareto Principle https://en.wikipedia.org/wiki/Pareto_principle

qTest https://www.tricentis.com/products/unified-test-management-qtest

TestRail https://www.testrail.com/

TestLink https://testlink.org/

Chapter 4

AI powered CI/CD pipeline improves time to delivery at Google:

https://devops.com/ai-powered-devops-transforming-ci-cd-pipelines-for-intelligent-automation/#:~:text=Notably%2C%20Google%20uses%20AI%20to,as%20conducting%20activities%20become%20efficient.

IBM uses AI In Software Development: https://www.ibm.com/think/topics/ai-in-software-develoment#:~:text=based%20on%20descriptions.-,Bug%20detection%20and%20fixing,time%20data%20to%20refine%20prototypes

RCA: Root Cause Analysis

Bug Triaging: Analysis of bugs to classify them with priorities (critical, high, medium, low) or associate them as showstoppers for a release or even as false positives.

Kaizen: Means Continuous Improvement. It is a Japanese word broken down into *'kai'* – continuous and *'zen'* – improvement.

Amazon uses AI to spot damaged products before they're shipped to customers

https://www.aboutamazon.com/news/innovation-at-amazon/amazon-ai-sustainability-carbon-footprint-product-defects

Netflix Data Pipeline: https://netflixtechblog.com/data-pipeline-asset-management-with-dataflow-86525b3e21ca

Chapter 5

ContextQA leverages IBM's watsonx.ai to expedite DevOps: https://contextqa.com/contextqa-leverages-ibm-to-expedite-devops/

Amazon Applicant Tracking System: https://www.reuters.com/article/us-amazon-com-jobs-automation-insight-idUSKCN1MK08G

IBM Watson's Approach to AI Bias in Software Testing https://www.ibm.com/think/topics/shedding-light-on-ai-bias-with-real-world-examples

Amazon DevOps Guru: https://aws.amazon.com/devops-guru/

DevOps Guru Blog Post: https://blog.searce.com/aws-devops-guru-an-overview-62877ffedb7

Amazon GuardDuty: https://aws.amazon.com/guardduty/

Netflix and its AI powered automation for video streaming services, an article:

https://www.bestpractice.ai/ai-case-study-best-practice/netflix_increases_quality_control_efficiency_by_using_machine_learning_to_predict_which_video_assets_are_likely_to_fail

Chapter 6

IBM's AI-Powered Automation Framework: https://www.ibm.com/automation#:~:text=IBM%20Automation-,IBM%20Automation,enhances%20performance%2C%20productivity%20and%20collaboration.&text=Automating%20Application%20Resource%20Management%20for,decisions%20and%20optimize%20cloud%20spend.

Microsoft Power Automate: https://www.microsoft.com/en-us/power-platform/products/power-automate

Aplitools Visual Testing: https://applitools.com/blog/visual-testing/

Testim: https://www.testim.io/test-automation-tool/

Mendix: https://www.mendix.com/evaluation-guide/app-lifecycle/develop/test-automation-quality-assurance/

OutSystems: https://www.outsystems.com/blog/posts/launching-the-quality-apps-program/

Chapter 7

Snyk: https://snyk.io/articles/vulnerability-scanner/

Checkmarx: https://checkmarx.com/

IBM Watsonx AI for cyber security: https://www.ndtvprofit.com/technology/ibm-introduces-gen-ai-powered-cybersecurity-assistant-for-threat-detection-and-response

Netflix Chaos Monkey & Simian Army: https://netflixtechblog.com/the-netflix-simian-army-16e57fbab116

DevSecOps: DevSecOps, short for Development, Security, and Operations, is a framework that integrates security practices into every stage of the software development lifecycle, fostering collaboration between development, security, and operations teams to build secure applications efficiently.

BeyondCorp: https://cloud.google.com/beyondcorp

Chapter 8

Basiri, A., et al. (2016). Chaos Engineering. *Netflix Technology Blog*. Retrieved from https://netflixtechblog.com/chaos-engineering-building-confidence-in-system-behavior-through-experimentation-914f1f6a9e31

Gremlin Chaos Engineering Platform: https://www.gremlin.com

LitmusChaos: https://litmuschaos.io

Microsoft Power Apps Documentation: https://learn.microsoft.com/en-us/power-apps/

OutSystems Low-Code Platform: https://www.outsystems.com/

Chapter 9

Testim: https://www.testim.io/test-automation-tool/

Mabl: https://www.mabl.com/

AI-Driven Test Prioritization at at Google to reduce execution time in its CI/CD pipelines: https://cloud.google.com/blog/topics/developers-practitioners/boost-your-continuous-delivery-pipeline-with-generative-ai

Aplitools Visual AI: https://applitools.com/platform/validate/visual-ai/

Article on effortless programming (by Eric Elliot): https://medium.com/effortless-programming/the-ai-driven-development-glossary-a487616801b6

Sapiesnz AI at Facebook: https://engineering.fb.com/2018/05/02/developer-tools/sapienz-intelligent-automated-software-testing-at-scale/

AI-Powered Testing Framework at Amazon: https://aws.amazon.com/blogs/security/generate-ai-powered-insights-for-amazon-security-lake-using-amazon-sagemaker-studio-and-amazon-bedrock/

Chapter 10

TestRigor: https://testrigor.com/

Functionize: https://www.functionize.com/

AI-based Defect Triaging (ADT*): https://www.virtusa.com/insights/perspectives/automated-defect-triaging

chapter 11: Timeless!! The Time Is Now

Robbins, T. (1991). *Awaken the Giant Within*. Free Press.

Hardy, D. (2010). *The Compound Effect*. Success Books.

Robbins, M. (2017). *The 5 Second Rule*. Savio Republic.

Maxwell, J. C. (2007). *The 21 Irrefutable Laws of Leadership*. Thomas Nelson.

Ziglar, Z. (1992). *See You at the Top*. Pelican Publishing.